MW01154795

The Story of the Dallas Cowboys and That Big Texas Town

By David and Daniel Hellman
Illustrated by Ronald Allan Ladlad

Many, many years ago,
folks in Dallas could only dream...

That someday they would cheer for their
very own pro football team...

Finally in 1960 the dreams
of that Big Texas Town came true...

As the Dallas fans could now cheer for
a team wearing silver and blue...

Yes a new football team for Dallas
was added to the game

But they had yet to decide what
would be their name?

The fans argued and debated,
but above all the noise

One fan stood and asked
"How about... the Cowboys?"

And at the first game the fans cheered,
"Well would you look at that!"

"A field full of Cowboys... and a man in a hat!"

The team was young and would not win right away,

But Coach Landry would corral them
and teach them to play.

The team needed someone
to throw the long bomb.

So Coach Landry found Meredith,
the original Cowboy... Dandy Don.

The Cowboys struggled against teams
from the East and the West.

These players looked more like greenhorns,
and not as good as the rest.

And the Cowboys, they lost most every game,

But their fans from that Big Texas Town
came to cheer just the same.

In their first years,
the wins were as rare as a
Texas snow.

But with grit and determination,
a glimmer of greatness
started to show.

Then... the Cowboys began to beat the
teams from the East and the West,

And that Big Texas Town soon realized,
their team was one of the best.

And the wins they kept coming
for **20** straight years,

So many celebrations...
and very few tears.

And working so hard made the victories so nice

Reaching five Super Bowls, and winning it twice.

Year in and year out to their foes they gave a hurtin'

Only coming up short when running into a **Steel Curtain**.

Soon other teams noticed when the
Cowboys rode into town,

The stands were filled with silver and blue...
and cowboy hats all around.

And through the thick
and even the thin,

The Cowboys would somehow,
find a way to win.

Like up in frosty Minnesota when
things got scary,

Captain Comeback said a prayer and
threw up a Hail Mary.

And on days when the offense struggled to play,

The team could rely on their defense... DOOMSDAY!!!"

And through it all our Cowboys
did not break nor bend,

But after 20 winning seasons,
their good fortune came to an end.

All the great players and coaches would gradually leave,

As the fans waved goodbye and wiped a tear with their sleeve.

Then...

They had a losing season,
and began losing year after year,

But that Big Texas Town
loved their Cowboys and
still came to cheer.

Finally, after all the great memories, including the Hail Mary,

The fans now welcomed
a new coach and
an owner named Jerry.

The two got together and developed a scheme.

"We'll trade our best player and build up our team."

The fans thought
they were crazy.
They could not see.

But along with the new
players emerged
the Big Three.

Coach Johnson demanded greatness.
He would settle for nothing less.

And the players worked hard
to give him their best.

With explosive players and
the best offensive line around

Victories and greatness soon
returned to that Big Texas Town.

After just a few years
these Cowboys were back.

This team was loaded.
There was no doubt about that.

Then...

**They beat a team from the East
and another from the West,**

**Letting everyone know
they were again one of the best.**

Off to the Super Bowl with one game to play

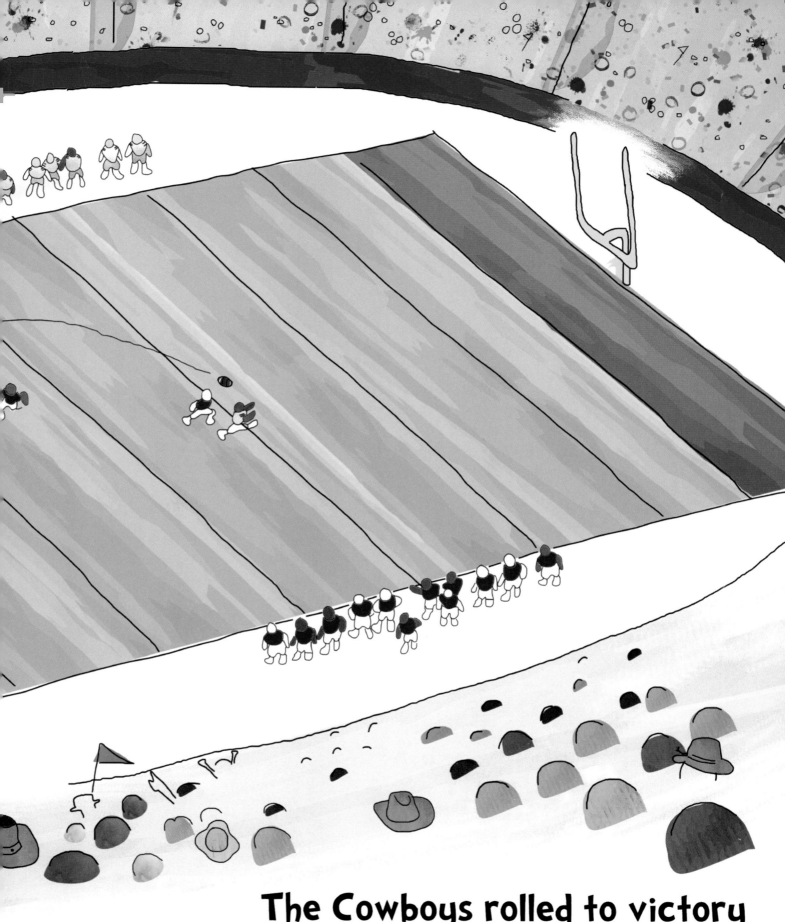

The Cowboys rolled to victory
and made the fans day

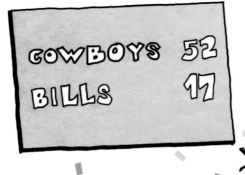

Above the celebration,
above all the noise,

Coach Johnson shouted to all
"How 'bout them Cowboys!!!"

The Texas-sized celebration
lasted until the next season came.

And woudn't you know it, at the
next Super Bowl, the result was the same.

And just to show that their greatness was certain
Just two Super Bowls later, they even
beat the Steel Curtain

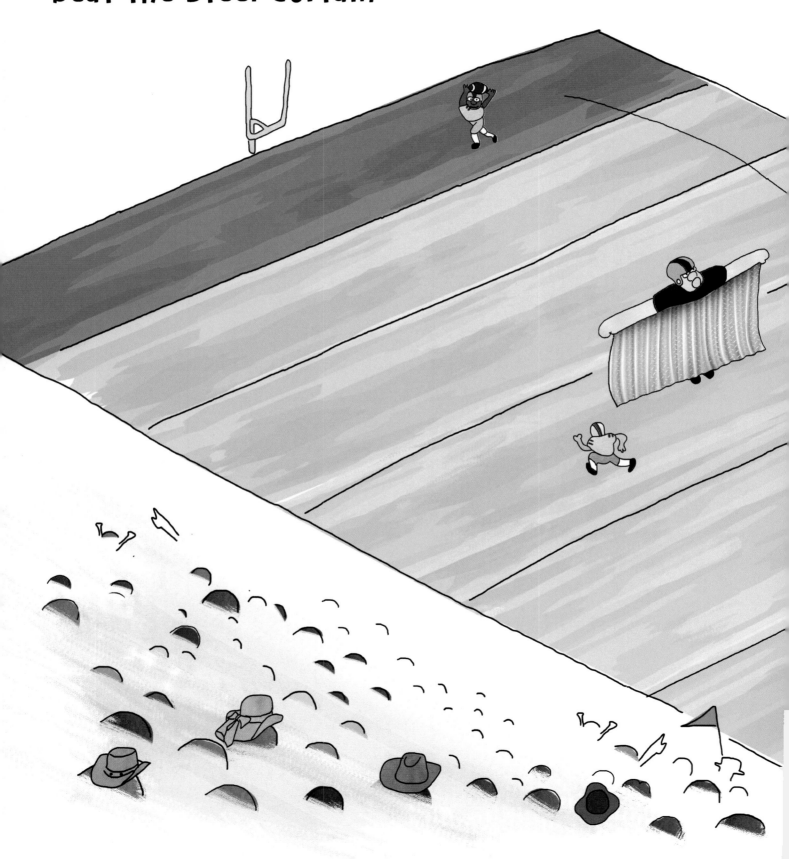

And while the Cowboys
cannot be champs every year,

Their fans... True Cowboy fans...
will always be there to cheer.

To this very day,
that Big Texas Town cheers
for the silver and blue.

So let this be your guide
in whatever you do.

If greatness is your goal,
if excellence is your dream,

Always remember the
Dallas Cowboys...
America's Team.

Made in the USA
Middletown, DE
04 February 2022